GOLF INSTRUCTION HANDBOOK FOR BEGINNERS

Master the Rules, Perfect Your Grip, the Intricacies of Swing Mechanics, and Nuances Of Course Etiquette

Henrietta J. Neil

TABLE OF CONTENTS

Introduction

In the quaint town of Greenview, nestled between rolling hills and lush greens, lived a young man named Alex. The allure of golf had always captivated him; the elegance of the swing, the precision of the putt, and the tranquility of the vast fairways called out to him like an enchanting melody. However, for Alex, who had never held a golf club in his life, the sport seemed as mysterious and elusive as a hidden treasure.

Every afternoon, he would pass by the majestic golf course on his way home from work, his eyes drawn to the players in their crisp attire, confidently striding from one hole to the next. They seemed to possess a mastery of the game that was beyond his wildest dreams. Alex yearned to join their ranks, but he was met with the unyielding reality of his beginner status.

One serendipitous day, as Alex wandered through a quaint secondhand bookstore on a whim, he stumbled upon a book neatly tucked away in a corner. Its title, "Golf Instruction Handbook," beckoned to him like a guiding light. Intrigued, he dusted off the cover and turned the pages, revealing a world of secrets waiting to be unlocked.

The book promised to be a beacon for aspiring golfers, illuminating the path from the uncharted waters of novices to the glistening greens of proficiency. Its pages contained an abundance of knowledge, from the fundamentals of grip and stance to the intricacies of swing mechanics and the nuances of course etiquette. It also contains Over 35 recommended exercises for beginners to achieve fitness and be in their best form and weight training workouts for beginners. With every word he read, Alex felt the veil of uncertainty lifting, replaced by a newfound sense of determination.

As he devoured each chapter, Alex found himself immersed in the journey of a lifetime. He learned the significance of the grip, the art of reading the greens, and the rhythm of a perfect swing. The book was not merely a manual; it was a mentor, offering insight and wisdom from seasoned players who had once stood in his shoes.

With each passing day, Alex honed his skills on the driving range and practiced his putting until the stars shimmered in the night sky. As he absorbed the lessons within the pages, he began to feel a sense of camaraderie with the golfing greats of the past, as if their spirits were guiding him toward his dreams.

Today, Alex stands among the great players in the game. The once bewildering sport has transformed into a cherished passion, a journey that has sculpted him into a golfer filled with both skill and grace. The book, now dog-eared and cherished, has become his constant companion, a testament to his triumph over uncertainty and a bridge to his aspirations.

And now, dear reader, you too hold in your hands the very book that led Alex on his extraordinary odyssey. "Golf Instruction Handbook for Beginners" is more than just a guide; it is a roadmap to unlocking the potential within you, transporting you from the realms of inexperience to the majesty of the greens. Whether you're a seasoned golfer seeking to fine-tune your game or a newcomer with a desire to learn, this book promises to be your trusted companion, just as it was for Alex. Let the journey begin.

Golf Basics:

Golf is a precision sport played on a course with 9 or 18 holes. Each hole has a designated tee box, a fairway, a rough, and a green with a flagstick. The objective of the game is to hit a golf ball from the tee box into the hole on the green in as few strokes as possible. At the conclusion of the round, the person with the least number of points is the victor.

Golf Rules

Understanding and following the rules of golf is essential for fair play and maintaining the integrity of the game. Some of the key rules include:

- **Play the ball as it lies:** Players must play the ball from wherever it comes to rest, whether it's in the fairway, rough, sand bunker, or on the green. Exceptions include certain relief situations, like when the ball is unplayable or stuck in a dangerous position.

- **Playing Order:** The player furthest from the hole plays first on each shot. This order is maintained throughout the hole, starting from the tee box.

- **Out of Bounds:** If your ball goes out of bounds (beyond the course boundaries), you must take a penalty stroke and replay the shot from the previous spot where you played the shot.

- **Water Hazards:** If your ball lands in a water hazard (marked with yellow or red stakes or lines), you have the option to play the ball as it lies with a penalty stroke or take a drop away from the hazard with an additional penalty stroke.

- **Lost Ball:** If you can't find your ball within three minutes of searching, it is considered lost, and you must take a penalty stroke and replay from the previous spot.

Golf Etiquette

Golf etiquette is all about showing respect to fellow players, the golf course, and the game itself. Some key points include:

- **Quiet and Still:** When someone is taking a shot, be quiet and stand still. Any unnecessary noise or movement can distract the player.

- **Repair Divots and Ball Marks:** After taking a shot, always repair any divots (chunks of turf) and ball marks on the green. This helps maintain the course and provides a smoother putting surface for others.
- **Walking in Putting Line:** Avoid walking on the line between the ball and the hole on the green. Footprints can affect the ball's path, so be cautious and walk around the line.
- **Pace of Play:** Play at a reasonable pace to keep the game moving. If your group is significantly slower than the group ahead, allow faster groups to play through.
- **Respect for Others:** Be courteous and respectful to other golfers. Don't talk or make noise during their swings, and offer compliments on good shots.

Putting

Putting is one of the most critical aspects of golf since it can significantly impact your score. Here are some putting tips:

- **Read the Green:** Before putting, take a few practice swings and study the slope and breaks of the green.

Look for subtle changes in elevation that could affect the ball's path.

- **Steady Grip:** Hold the putter with a relaxed and steady grip. Avoid gripping too tightly, as this can cause tension and affect your stroke.

- **Pendulum-like Stroke:** For a smooth putting stroke, imagine swinging the putter like a pendulum. Let the motion come from your shoulders and maintain a consistent tempo.

- **Aim for Lag Putting:** On longer putts, aim to get the ball close to the hole rather than trying to sink it. This will reduce the chances of a three-putt and help you make a more manageable second putt.

Driving (Long Shots)

The driver is used for tee shots on long, open holes. For successful driving, here are some helpful tips:

- **Proper Tee Height:** Tee the ball at an appropriate height so that about half of the ball is above the top of the driver's face. This allows you to make solid contact with the sweet spot.

- **Eye on the Ball:** Keep your eye on the ball throughout the swing. Avoid the temptation to look up too early to see where the ball is going.

- **Fluid Swing:** Maintain a smooth, fluid swing to maximize clubhead speed and distance. Avoid swinging too hard, as this can lead to inconsistent shots.

- **Follow Through: After** making contact with the ball, complete your swing by extending the clubhead toward the target. A proper follow-through helps with accuracy and power.

Swinging (Irons)

Irons are used for intermediate distances and approach shots. Here are some tips for successful iron play:

- **Proper Alignment:** Align your body parallel to the target line. This helps ensure that the clubface is square to the target at impact.

- **Head Down, Eyes on the Ball:** Keep your head down and your eyes on the ball throughout the swing. This promotes better ball contact and accuracy.

- Divot Taking: For most iron shots, you should take a divot after impact with the ball. This means hitting the ball first and then the ground, which results in a clean strike.

- Club Selection: Know the distances you hit each iron and choose the appropriate club for the shot. Practice with different irons to get a feel for their distances.

Chipping

Chipping is a short, controlled shot used to get the ball close to the hole from around the green. Here are some chipping tips:

- **Club Selection:** Use a wedge or a short iron for chip shots. The loft on these clubs will help the ball get up in the air quickly and land softly.

- **Ball Position and Stance:** Position the ball back in your stance, closer to your back foot. Your weight should be slightly heavier on your front foot.

- **Short Swing:** Use a shorter backswing and follow-through for chip shots. The length of the backswing should be determined by the distance you want the ball to travel.

- **Let the Club Do the Work:** Avoid trying to lift the ball into the air. Instead, let the loft of the club do the work and allow the ball to roll out towards the hole.

Golf Tips for Beginners:

- **Take Lessons:** Consider taking lessons from a qualified golf instructor. They can teach you proper techniques and help you avoid developing bad habits from the start.

- **Practice Regularly:** Like any skill, golf improves with practice. Spend time at the driving range, practice putting green, and work on different aspects of your game.

- **Start with Shorter Courses:** Begin by playing on shorter and easier courses to build confidence and experience.

- **Enjoy the Game:** Golf can be challenging, but it's essential to have fun and enjoy the process of improvement.

- **Play with More Experienced Golfers:** Playing with more experienced golfers can provide valuable tips and insights. Observe their techniques and strategies.

- **Stay Positive:** Golf can be frustrating at times, but maintaining a positive attitude is crucial. Pay attention to your progress and take the time to recognize your accomplishments, no matter how minor.

Fundamentals of Grip and Stance

Grip

The grip is one of the most critical aspects of the golf swing, as it directly affects the clubface position at impact. There are three common grips: the overlapping grip, the interlocking grip, and the baseball grip. For beginners, the overlapping grip is often recommended. To achieve this grip:

- Hold the club with your left hand (for right-handed golfers) and wrap your fingers around the grip.
- Place your right hand over your left, with the pinky of your right hand resting between the index and middle fingers of your left hand.
- Your thumbs and index fingers should form a "V" shape, with the point of the "V" pointing towards your right shoulder.

Stance

A proper stance provides a stable foundation for your swing and ensures proper alignment. Follow these guidelines:

- Stand with your feet shoulder-width apart.

- Position the ball in line with the inside of your left heel (for right-handed golfers) for most shots.
- Slightly flare your feet outward to promote a natural rotation during the swing.
- Bend your legs a bit and lean your torso forward from the hips.

Intricacies of Swing Mechanics:

- **Takeaway:** Start the swing by moving the clubhead back along the target line, ensuring a smooth and controlled motion. Avoid jerking or lifting the club too quickly.
- **Backswing:** Rotate your torso while maintaining a stable lower body. Keep the club on the correct plane, allowing it to reach a horizontal position parallel to the ground.
- **Downswing:** Initiate the downswing with your lower body, shifting weight from the back foot to the front foot. Maintain a steady tempo and allow the club to follow a natural path toward the ball.
- **Impact:** At the moment of impact, the clubface should be square to the target line. Your weight

should be shifted to your front foot, and your hands should be slightly ahead of the ball.

- **Follow-Through:** Continue the swing with a smooth and balanced follow-through. Allow your body to rotate fully, facing the target with your chest and hips.

Nuances of Course Etiquette:

- **Respect the Game:** Golf is a sport built on etiquette and respect for fellow players, the course, and its traditions. Practice good sportsmanship and exhibit patience and courtesy toward others.

- **Pace of Play:** Play at a pace that keeps the flow of the game moving smoothly. Be prepared to take your shot when it's your turn, and try to avoid any delays.

- **Repair Divots and Ball Marks:** Replace divots or use sand to repair them. Additionally, repair any ball marks on the green to maintain its condition for other players.

- **Quiet and Stillness:** Maintain quiet and stillness while others are playing their shots. Sudden movements or noises can be distracting to players during their swings.

- **Stay on Cart Paths:** If using a golf cart, observe course rules and stay on designated cart paths, especially near tees, greens, and areas with wet conditions.

- **Safety First:** Always be mindful of the safety of yourself and others. Never swing a club if someone is standing too close, and be aware of your surroundings on the course.

- **Dress Code:** Respect the dress code of the golf course you're playing on. Proper golf attire is typically required, including collared shirts and golf shoes.

- **Cell Phones:** Keep cell phones on silent mode and use them sparingly, especially on the course. Avoid talking on the phone during play.

- **Raking Bunkers:** After hitting a shot from a bunker, use a rake to smooth the sand to leave it in good condition for other players.

- **Maintain Pace:** Keep up with the group ahead of you and let faster groups play through if your group is falling behind.

40 Fitness and Best Performance Exercises for Beginners

Here are 40 exercises that are recommended for golfers, along with instructions and the health benefits of each exercise:

1. Core Rotations:

Instructions:

- Stand with your feet shoulder-width apart, holding a light medicine ball or weight plate.
- Rotate your torso from side to side, engaging your core muscles with each rotation.

Health Benefits:

- This exercise helps to improve rotational power and stability in the golf swing.
- It also enhances core strength for better balance and control.

2. Medicine Ball Woodchoppers:

Instructions:

- Stand with your feet shoulder-width apart while holding a medicine ball in both hands.
- Swing the ball diagonally across your body from high to low, engaging your core and oblique muscles.
- **Health Benefits:**
- This exercise develops core strength and rotational power for an efficient golf swing.
- It also works the oblique muscles, which are essential for generating torque during the swing.

3. Seated Trunk Rotations:

Instructions:

- Sit on a stable chair or bench, holding a golf club behind your neck.
- Keeping your hips stable, rotate your upper body from side to side.

Health Benefits:

- This exercise increases flexibility and range of motion in the upper body.
- It also helps to prevent injuries and improve posture during the golf swing.

4. Hip Rotations:

Instructions:

- Lie on your back, with your feet flat on the floor and your knees bent.
- Let your knees fall to one side, then the other, while keeping your upper back on the ground.

Health Benefits:

- This exercise enhances hip mobility and flexibility, which are crucial for a fluid golf swing.
- It also reduces the risk of lower back pain and improves hip rotation during the swing.

5. Glute Bridges:

Instructions:

- Lie on your back, with your feet flat on the floor and your knees bent.
- Squeezing your glutes at the top, raise your hips off the ground.

Health Benefits:

- This exercise strengthens the glutes, which are essential for stability and power during the swing.
- It also helps to maintain proper posture and alignment during the golf swing.

6. Single-Leg Deadlifts:

Instructions:

- Maintain a small bend in your knee while you balance on one leg.
- Hinge at the hips, lowering your upper body while extending the opposite leg behind you.

Health Benefits:

- This exercise improves balance, stability, and single-leg strength.
- It also develops hamstring and glute strength for better control in the golf swing.

7. Squats:

Instructions:

- With your toes turned out slightly and your feet shoulder-width apart, stand.

- Maintain a straight back, bend at the knees and hips to lower your body.

Health Benefits:

- This exercise builds leg strength and power for generating clubhead speed.
- It also engages the core and stabilizes muscles for improved balance.

8. Lunges:

Instructions:

- Stand with your feet hip-width apart.
- With one leg, advance one step, then squat down until both knees are at a 90-degree angle.

Health Benefits:

- This exercise strengthens the legs and improves balance and stability.
- It also works the hip flexors and quadriceps for better movement in the golf swing.

9. Planks:

Instructions:

- To start, perform a push-up with your forearms on the ground.
- Keep your body in a straight line from your head to your heels by using your core muscles.

Health Benefits:

- This exercise builds core strength and stability for better control during the golf swing.
- It also engages the entire body for improved overall fitness.

10. Side Planks:

Instructions:

- Stack your legs while lying on your side with your elbow directly beneath your shoulder.
- Lift your hips off the floor and maintain a straight line from your head to your heels.

Health Benefits:

- This exercise increases lateral stability while working the oblique muscles.

- It also enhances core strength and balance during the golf swing.

11. Push-Ups:

Instructions:

- Start out in a plank position with your hands slightly wider than shoulder-width apart. Your chest should be virtually touching the ground when you flex your elbows.

Health Benefits:

- Push-ups help build upper body and core strength for better club control and stability. They also target the chest, shoulders, and triceps for a more balanced physique.

12. Pull-Ups or Assisted Pull-Ups:

Instructions:

- Use a pull-up bar or a resistance band for assistance. Your chin should be above the bar as you lift your body up.

Health Benefits:

- Pull-ups strengthen the upper back and arms for better control of the club during the swing. They also engage the core and improve grip strength for a more powerful swing.

13. Shoulder External Rotations:

Instructions:

- Fasten a resistance band to a fixed object at waist height. Stand sideways to the anchor point with your elbow bent 90 degrees.

Health Benefits:

- Shoulder external rotations target the rotator cuff muscles, which are essential for shoulder stability during the golf swing. They also help prevent shoulder injuries and improve shoulder range of motion.

14. Dumbbell Rows:

Instructions:

- Place one hand and one knee on a bench, holding a dumbbell in the opposite hand. Pull the dumbbell upward toward your hip, squeezing your shoulder blades together.

Health Benefits:

- Dumbbell rows target the upper back muscles for better posture and shoulder stability. They also engage the core and improve balance during the rowing motion.

15. Shoulder Press:

Instructions:

- Holding dumbbells at shoulder height, stand with your feet shoulder-width apart. Raise the dumbbells overhead once your arms are completely stretched.

Health Benefits:

Shoulder presses strengthen the shoulder muscles for improved club control and stability. They also engage the core and improve upper body strength.

16. Calf Raises:

Instructions:

- For balance, stand with your feet hip-width apart, close to a wall or other stable surface. Stand up straight on your toes, and lift your heels off the ground.

Health Benefits:

- Calf raises strengthen the calf muscles for better stability and balance during the golf swing. They also target the lower leg muscles for a more powerful push-off during the swing.

17. Cardiovascular Exercise:

Instructions:

- Engage in cardiovascular activities like brisk walking, jogging, cycling, or swimming.

Health Benefits:

- Cardiovascular exercise improves cardiovascular endurance for better performance throughout the round. It also increases stamina and mental focus during the game.

18. Flexibility Exercises:

Instructions:

- Incorporate stretching exercises like shoulder stretches, hip stretches, and hamstring stretches.

Health Benefits:

- Flexibility exercises improve flexibility and range of motion in key areas for the golf swing. Additionally, they ease muscle tension and aid in injury prevention.

19. Balance Exercises:

Instructions:

- Include exercises that challenge your balance, such as single-leg stands, balance board exercises, or stability ball exercises.

Health Benefits:

- Balance exercises improve stability and proprioception, which are critical for a consistent and accurate golf swing. They also enhance overall body control and coordination.

20. Warm-Up and Cool-Down:

Instructions:

- Before you start your golf fitness routine, always warm up to get your blood flowing and your body ready for exercise.

- Finish with a cool-down, including some light stretching, to help with flexibility and aid in recovery.

Health Benefits:

- Warming up and cooling down reduces the risk of injury by gradually increasing blood flow and body temperature.

- It also helps to prevent post-exercise muscle soreness and stiffness.

21. Side Lunges:

Instructions:

- Stand with your feet hip-width apart.

- Take a broad step to the side while maintaining the other leg straight and bending the knee of the lunging leg.

- Repeat on the opposite side after pushing back to the beginning position.

Health Benefits:

- This exercise targets the inner and outer thigh muscles, enhancing stability and lateral movement.
- It also helps to improve lower body strength for better weight transfer during the golf swing.

22. Stability Ball Rollouts:

Instructions:

- Kneel with your hands on a stability ball in front of you.
- Roll the ball forward, extending your arms and keeping your body in a straight line from head to knees.
- To return the ball to the starting location, use your core.

Health Benefits:

- This exercise engages the core muscles for better stability and balance during the golf swing.

- It also strengthens the shoulders and upper body for improved club control.

23. Lateral Band Walks:

Instructions:

- Put a resistance band around your ankles.
- Keeping tension in the band, take small steps sideways.

Health Benefits:

- This exercise targets the hip abductor muscles, which are essential for lateral movement in the golf swing.
- It also helps to improve hip and glute strength for better weight transfer and balance.

24. Russian Twists:

Instructions:

- Kneel down with your feet flat on the ground.
- Lean back slightly and twist your torso from side to side, touching the ground with your hands.

Health Benefits:

- This exercise works the oblique muscles and improves core rotation for an efficient golf swing.
- It also enhances balance and control during rotational movements.

25. Lateral Dumbbell Raises:

Instructions:

- Firmly holding dumbbells in your hand, stand with your feet shoulder-width apart.
- Raise the dumbbells out to the sides until they are parallel to the ground.
- Lower the dumbbells back down and repeat for a set of repetitions.

Health Benefits:

- This exercise targets the deltoid muscles for better shoulder stability during the golf swing.
- It also engages the upper back and improves posture.

26. Hamstring Curls:

Instructions:

- Lie face down on a stability ball or bench with your hips on the edge.

- Bend your knees and lift your heels toward your glutes, squeezing your hamstrings.

- Lower your legs again, and repeat over and over again.

Health Benefits:

- This exercise strengthens the hamstrings for better control during the swing and reduces the risk of hamstring injuries.

- It also engages the glutes and improves hip extension for a more powerful swing.

27. Stability Ball Pike Rollouts:

Instructions:

- Begin by doing a push-up while standing on a stability ball with your shins.

- Lifting your hips into a pike stance, engage your core as you roll the ball toward your chest.

- Roll the ball back to the starting position and repeat for a set of repetitions.

Health Benefits:

- This exercise challenges the core and improves stability and balance during dynamic movements.
- It also enhances shoulder and upper body strength for better control of the club.

28. Quadruped Leg Lifts:

Instructions:

- Get into a quadruped position on your hands and knees.
- Maintaining alignment with your body, lift one leg straight back.
- Reverse the process on the other side by lowering the leg again.

Health Benefits:

- Strengthening the glutes and hamstrings helps with hip extension during the golf swing.
- Improves core stability and control during single-leg movements.

29. Banded Hip Abduction:

Instructions:

- Secure a resistance band around your ankles.
- Stand with your feet shoulder-width apart and step sideways, stretching the band.
- Go back to your starting position, and repeat on the other side.

Health Benefits:

- This exercise targets the hip abductor muscles, improving lateral movement and stability.
- Engages the glutes and hip muscles for better weight transfer during the swing.

30. Side Plank with Leg Lift:

Instructions:

- Begin in a side plank position with your elbow directly beneath your shoulder.
- Lift the top leg toward the ceiling, keeping your hips and body stable.
- Lower the leg back down and repeat for a set of repetitions.

Health Benefits:

- Engages the obliques and lateral hip muscles for improved stability and rotation in the golf swing.
- Challenges core strength and balance during the leg lift.

31. Standing Calf Raises:

Instructions:

- Stand with feet hip-width apart near a wall or sturdy surface for balance.
- Stand up straight on your toes by lifting your heels off the ground.
- Lower your heels back down and repeat for a set of repetitions.

Health Benefits:

- This exercise targets the calf muscles for better balance and stability during the golf swing.
- Enhances ankle strength and flexibility for a more fluid swing.

32. Stability Ball Hip Bridge:

Instructions:

- Lie on your back with your feet on a stability ball, knees bent.
- Squeeze your glutes at the peak as you raise your hips toward the ceiling.
- Lower your hips back down and repeat for a set of repetitions.

Health Benefits:

- Strengthens the glutes and hamstrings for better hip extension and stability.
- Engages the core for improved pelvic control during the golf swing.

33. Plank to Push-Up:

Instructions:

- On your forearms, start in a plank position.
- Push up onto your hands into a push-up position.
- Return to the plank position on your forearms and repeat for a set of repetitions.

Health Benefits:

- This exercise targets the chest, shoulders, and triceps for upper body strength and control.
- Engages the core and shoulders for stability during the push-up and plank transitions.

34. Scapular Retractions:

Instructions:

- You can sit or stand with both arms at your sides.
- Squeeze your shoulder blades together, pulling them down toward your back pockets.
- Hold for a few seconds, and then release.

Health Benefits:

- Improves scapular stability and control for better posture and shoulder mobility during the golf swing.
- Reduces the risk of shoulder injuries and enhances upper back strength.

35. Banded Face Pulls:

Instructions:

- At chest height, fasten a resistance band to the object.

- Hold the band with both hands and pull it toward your face, squeezing your shoulder blades together.
- Slowly release and repeat for a set of repetitions.

Health Benefits:

- This exercise targets the rear deltoid and upper back muscles for better shoulder stability and control.
- Engages the upper back and improves posture during the golf swing.

36. Single-Leg Balance with Dumbbell Press:

Instructions:

- Stand on one leg, holding a dumbbell in the opposite hand at shoulder height.
- Press the dumbbell overhead while maintaining balance on one leg.
- Lower the dumbbell back down and repeat for a set of repetitions.

Health Benefits:

- This exercise challenges balance and stability during the single-leg stance and dumbbell press.

- Engages the core, shoulders, and upper body for better control and coordination.

37. Stability Ball Stir the Pot:

Instructions:

- Start in a plank position with your forearms on a stability ball.
- Move the ball in small circles in one direction, then switch directions.

Health Benefits:

- Engages the core, shoulders, and stabilizing muscles for improved balance and control.
- Targets the entire upper body and core for a functional and challenging exercise.

38. Lateral Lunge with Medicine Ball Rotation:

Instructions:

- A medicine ball should be held in front of your chest.
- Take a broad step to the side while maintaining the other leg straight and bending the knee of the lunging leg.

- Rotate your torso toward the lunging leg, then return to the starting position.

Health Benefits:

- Enhances lateral movement and stability in the golf swing.

- Develops rotational power and core strength with the added medicine ball rotation.

39. TRX Row:

Instructions:

- Set up a TRX suspension trainer at waist height.

- Walk your feet forward until your body is at an angle while holding the handles with your hands facing in.

- Squeeze your shoulder blades together as you pull your chest toward the handles.

- Lower your body back down and repeat for a set of repetitions.

Health Benefits:

- Targets the upper back and biceps for better shoulder stability and control.

- Engages the core and improves overall upper body strength.

40. Split Squat Jumps:

Instructions:

- Start in a split squat position with one foot forward and the other foot back.
- Lower your body into a lunge, then explode up and switch legs in mid-air.
- Land softly in the opposite split squat position and repeat for a set of repetitions.

Health Benefits:

- Develops lower body power and explosiveness for a more dynamic golf swing.
- Challenges balance and coordination during the split squat jump.

Health Benefits of Golf-Focused Fitness

- **Improved Flexibility:** Enhanced flexibility leads to a more fluid golf swing and reduces the risk of injuries, such as strains and sprains.

- **Increased Strength:** Building strength in key muscle groups improves stability, control, and power during the golf swing.

- **Enhanced Balance:** Better balance aids in maintaining proper posture and weight transfer throughout the swing.

- **Core Stability:** A strong core is essential for generating rotational power and maintaining control during the swing.

- **Injury Prevention:** A well-rounded fitness routine helps prevent common golf-related injuries and overuse issues.

- **Stamina and Endurance:** Golfers who have better stamina and cardiovascular fitness are better able to stay focused and perform consistently throughout the round.

- **Better Mental Focus:** Regular exercise and physical fitness contribute to improved mental focus and concentration on the golf course.

- **Overall Health and Wellness:** Engaging in golf-focused fitness contributes to overall health and well-being, promoting longevity and a higher quality of life.

It's important to note that before starting any exercise program, it's advisable to consult with a fitness professional or healthcare provider, especially if you have any pre-existing medical conditions or injuries. Additionally, ensure that you use proper form and technique during all exercises to minimize the risk of injury and maximize the benefits. A comprehensive golf-specific fitness routine can help golfers achieve their best form, improve performance, and enjoy the game to the fullest.

Weight Training for Golf for Beginners

Weight training can be beneficial for golfers, especially beginners, as it helps build strength, stability, and flexibility, all of which are important for improving their golf game. Weight training can enhance the power and control of the golf swing, reduce the risk of injuries, and contribute to better overall fitness. However, it's essential for beginners to approach weight training with proper form, appropriate exercises, and a gradual progression to avoid potential injuries.

Here are some important tips and guidelines for weight training for beginner golfers:

- **Start with a Warm-Up:** Before beginning any weight training session, warm up your body with dynamic stretches, light cardio, or bodyweight exercises. Warming up gets more blood into the muscles and gets them ready for the workout to come.

- **Focus on Functional Movements:** Opt for exercises that mimic the movements involved in the golf swing, such as rotational movements, core exercises, and movements that target the lower body and upper body muscles.

- **Begin with Bodyweight Exercises:** If you are new to weight training, start with bodyweight exercises to develop proper form and technique. Bodyweight exercises like squats, lunges, push-ups, and planks can help build a foundation of strength and stability.

- **Gradually Introduce Weights:** As you become more comfortable with bodyweight exercises, gradually introduce weights. Start with light weights and focus on maintaining proper form throughout each repetition.

- **Emphasize Core Training:** A strong core is essential for a stable and powerful golf swing. Include exercises like planks, Russian twists, and medicine ball rotations to target the core muscles.

- **Balance Upper and Lower Body Training:** Weight training should address both the upper and lower body muscles to maintain balance and symmetry in the golf swing. Include exercises like bicep curls, shoulder presses, and leg presses.

- **Perform Compound Movements:** Compound exercises work multiple muscle groups simultaneously and can be more effective for overall strength gains. Bench presses, squats, and deadlifts are a few examples.

- **Incorporate Rotational Exercises:** Golf is a rotational sport, so include exercises that target rotational power, such as cable chops, medicine ball throws, and dumbbell twists.

- **Focus on Controlled Movements:** Avoid using momentum to lift weights, as this can lead to improper form and potential injuries. Focus on controlled, deliberate movements throughout each exercise.

- **Allow for Rest and Recovery:** Weight training places stress on the muscles, so make sure to allow for adequate rest and recovery between sessions. Prior to working out the same muscle area again, try to give it at least 48 hours of rest.

- **Listen to Your Body:** If you experience any pain or discomfort during weight training, stop the exercise and seek guidance from a fitness professional or healthcare provider.

- **Progress Gradually:** As you become more experienced and comfortable with weight training, gradually increase the weight and intensity of your exercises. Avoid rapid increases to prevent overexertion or injuries.

- **Consistency is Key:** Consistency is essential for seeing progress in weight training. Aim for regular workouts, and remember that progress may be gradual, especially for beginners.

- **Combine Weight Training with Golf Practice:** Weight training should complement golf practice. Consider integrating golf-specific exercises and movements into your weight training routine.

- **Seek Professional Guidance:** If you are unsure where to start or need assistance with designing a weight training program tailored to your needs, consider working with a qualified fitness trainer who has experience with golf-specific training.

Remember that weight training is just one aspect of improving your golf game. Regular golf practice, along with a balanced fitness routine that includes cardiovascular exercise, flexibility training, and proper nutrition, will contribute to better performance and overall health on the golf course.

Conclusion

As you reach the final pages of "Golf Instruction Handbook for Beginners," I hope you feel equipped with the knowledge and confidence to embark on your golfing journey with enthusiasm and determination. The world of golf offers a treasure trove of experiences, and this book has been crafted to be your trusted companion, guiding you from the realm of uncertainty to the lush greens of proficiency.

Remember that every swing, every putt, and every round presents an opportunity for growth and improvement. Embrace the process, savor the victories, and learn from the challenges. With dedication and practice, you'll find yourself progressing from a beginner to a golfer of skill and grace.

I encourage you to share your experience with this book and the transformation it has ignited in your game. If you found "Golf Instruction Handbook for Beginners " to be a valuable resource on your golfing odyssey, please consider leaving a positive review. Your feedback can inspire and empower other golfing enthusiasts to discover their potential and set them on the path to success.

However, I must also highlight the importance of honest reviews. While I am confident that this book has been meticulously crafted to provide the utmost value, constructive criticism is equally valuable in shaping future editions. Negative reviews can have a significant impact on the reach and reputation of this book, potentially deterring other readers from experiencing the transformative journey you have undertaken.

Thank you for choosing "Golf Instruction Handbook for Beginners." I sincerely hope that it has kindled a love for the sport within you and that its teachings will resonate on every tee box, fairway, and green you encounter. May your golfing adventures be filled with joy, camaraderie, and the pursuit of excellence.

As you embark on this golfing expedition, I wish you fair winds, straight drives, and successful putts. May you forever find solace and exhilaration in the greens of this timeless sport.

Made in the USA
Las Vegas, NV
06 September 2024

94894786R00030